Contents

WHO WERE THE MAYA?

The Maya were people who lived in the forests of Central America. During their "Classic" period from around 250 to 900 CE, the Maya established powerful city-states, impressive architecture, religion, and writing.

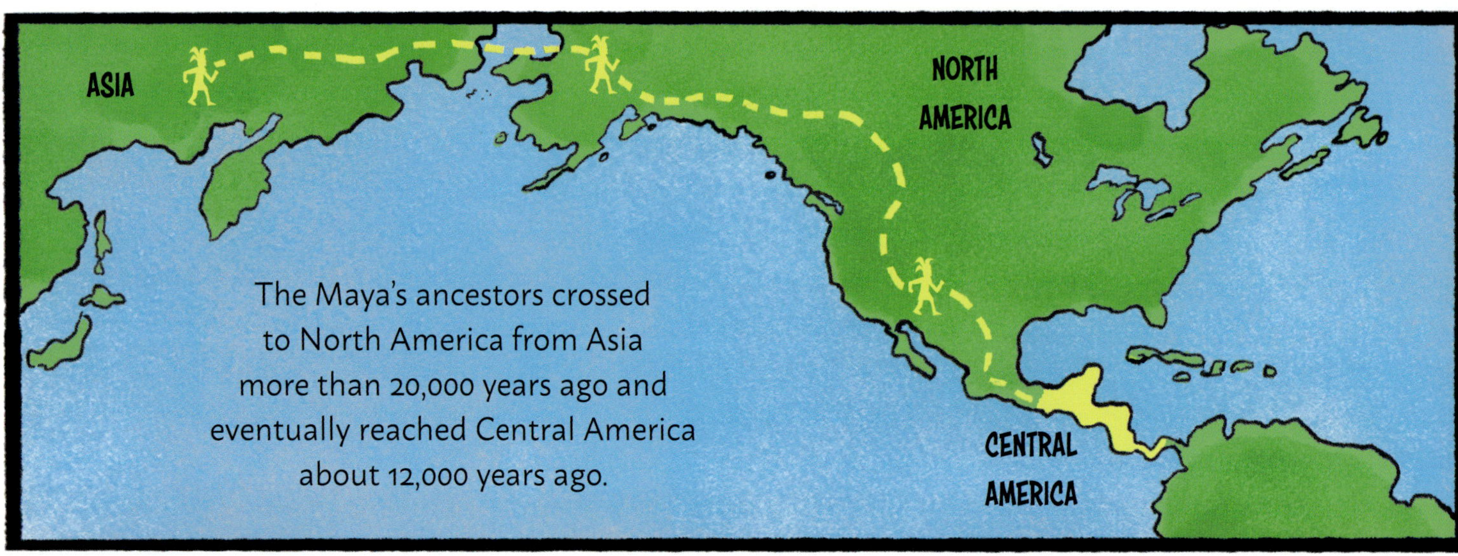

The Maya's ancestors crossed to North America from Asia more than 20,000 years ago and eventually reached Central America about 12,000 years ago.

Between 3,000 and 2,000 BCE , the Maya changed their lifestyle from hunting on the move to farming and settling down in villages.

From 2000 BCE to 250 CE (the "Preclassic" period), the Maya developed religious beliefs and erected monumental temples. They invented their system of writing and built their first cities.

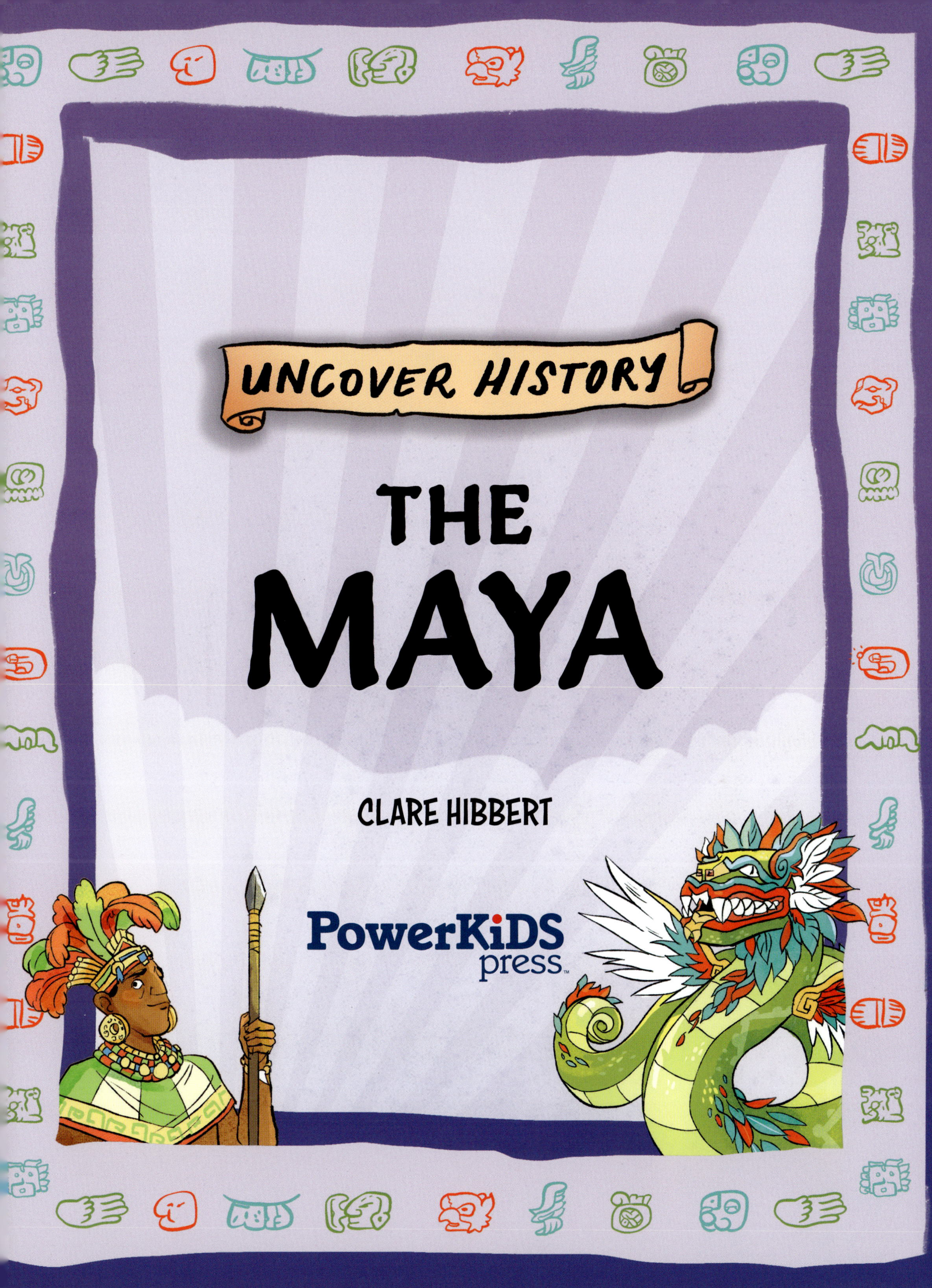

THE MAYA

CLARE HIBBERT

PowerKiDS press™

Published in 2026
by The Rosen Publishing Group, Inc.
2544 Clinton Street, Buffalo, NY 14224

First published in Great Britain in 2023 by Hodder & Stoughton
Copyright © Hodder & Stoughton Limited, 2023

Series Editor: Lisa Edwards
Series Design and illustration: Collaborate
Consultant: exicolore, a small independent teaching team providing specialist
educational services on Mexico and teaching resources on the Mexica (Aztecs) and Maya

The text in this book first appeared
in *History Detective Investigates: The Mayas* by Clare Hibbert (Wayland).

Cataloging-in-Publication Data
Names: Hibbert, Clare.
Title: The Maya / Clare Hibbert.
Description: Buffalo, NY : PowerKids Press, 2026. | Series: Uncover history | Includes glossary and index.
Identifiers: ISBN 9781499454543 (pbk.) | ISBN 9781499454550 (library bound) | ISBN 9781499454567 (ebook)
Subjects: LCSH:Mayas--Juvenile literature. | Mayas--Civilization--Juvenile literature. | Mayas--History--Juvenile literature.
| Mayas--Social life and customs--Juvenile literature.
Classification: LCC F1435.H533 2026 | DDC 972.81'016--dc23

Manufactured in the United States of America
CPSIA Compliance Information: Batch #CSPK26. For further information contact Rosen Publishing at 1-800-237-9932.

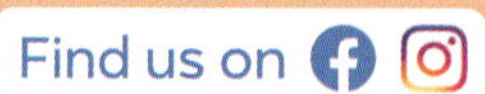

El Mirador (350 BCE–200 CE) may have had over 100,000 inhabitants. The city contains one of the earliest and largest Maya pyramids, the La Danta temple, at 230 feet (70 m) high.

Tikal city was most powerful in the Classic period (700s CE). In what is now northern Guatemala, it was ruled by a dynasty of kings.

Around 900 CE, Tikal, Copán, Palenque, and the other great cities were abandoned. Archaeologists are still not entirely sure why.

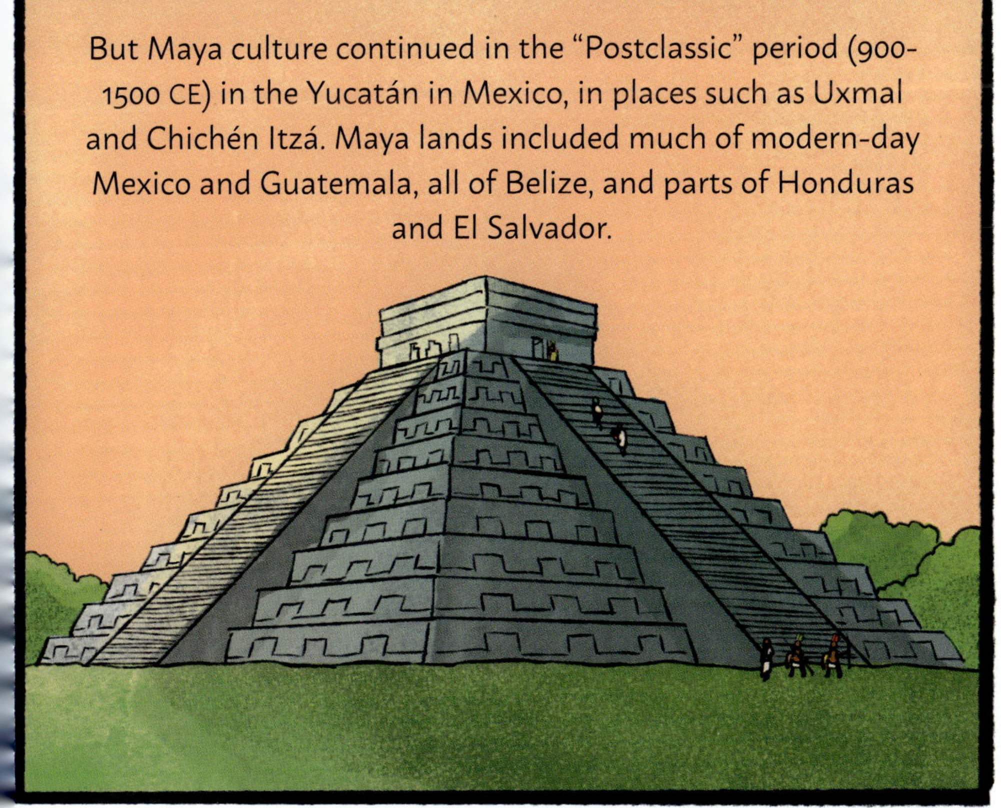

But Maya culture continued in the "Postclassic" period (900–1500 CE) in the Yucatán in Mexico, in places such as Uxmal and Chichén Itzá. Maya lands included much of modern-day Mexico and Guatemala, all of Belize, and parts of Honduras and El Salvador.

But great change came to the Maya with the arrival of Spanish explorers in the 1500s (see pages 26–27).

What Did Maya Farmers Grow?

Around 3500 BCE, the Maya began to grow maize. Before then, they had lived as hunter-gatherers, hunting animals and gathering roots, seeds, and fruit as they moved around. Now farmers, the Maya began to establish villages and city-states.

Maya farmers cleared fields in the rainforest using stone axes. Once they had chopped down most of the trees, they set fire to the remaining plant growth. This "slash-and-burn" technique produced ash to fertilize the soil.

The Maya realized they needed to give the land time to recover. They built terraces in hilly areas to stop soil from slipping away during heavy rain and dug channels to carry water to where the land was dry.

Besides maize, the Maya planted beans, squash, peppers, sweet potatoes, tomatoes, and cassava. They also grew breadnut, avocado, and papaya trees and even kept bees for honey.

The Maya gathered cacao beans and made a bitter chocolate drink from them, as well as using them as "money."

Maize was their most important crop. Tortillas accompanied every meal and were baked on a stone over an open fire. Maize was also turned into porridge.

The Maya continued to hunt deer, peccaries (pig-like animals), and tapirs in the forest but they also kept turkeys. Dogs sometimes helped with hunting but others were fattened up to be sacrificed (see pages 14-15).

How Many City-States Were There?

The Maya developed more than 60 city-states, which had their own kings and, in a few cases, queens, but shared the same culture, language and beliefs. Sometimes smaller city-states came under the control of larger, more powerful ones.

Archaeologists have uncovered the remains of many Maya settlements across Guatemala and Mexico, including Tikal, Calakmul, Palenque, Caracol, Copán, and Yaxchilan. Maya merchants traveled between these cities (see pages 24-25), some of which were connected by roads.

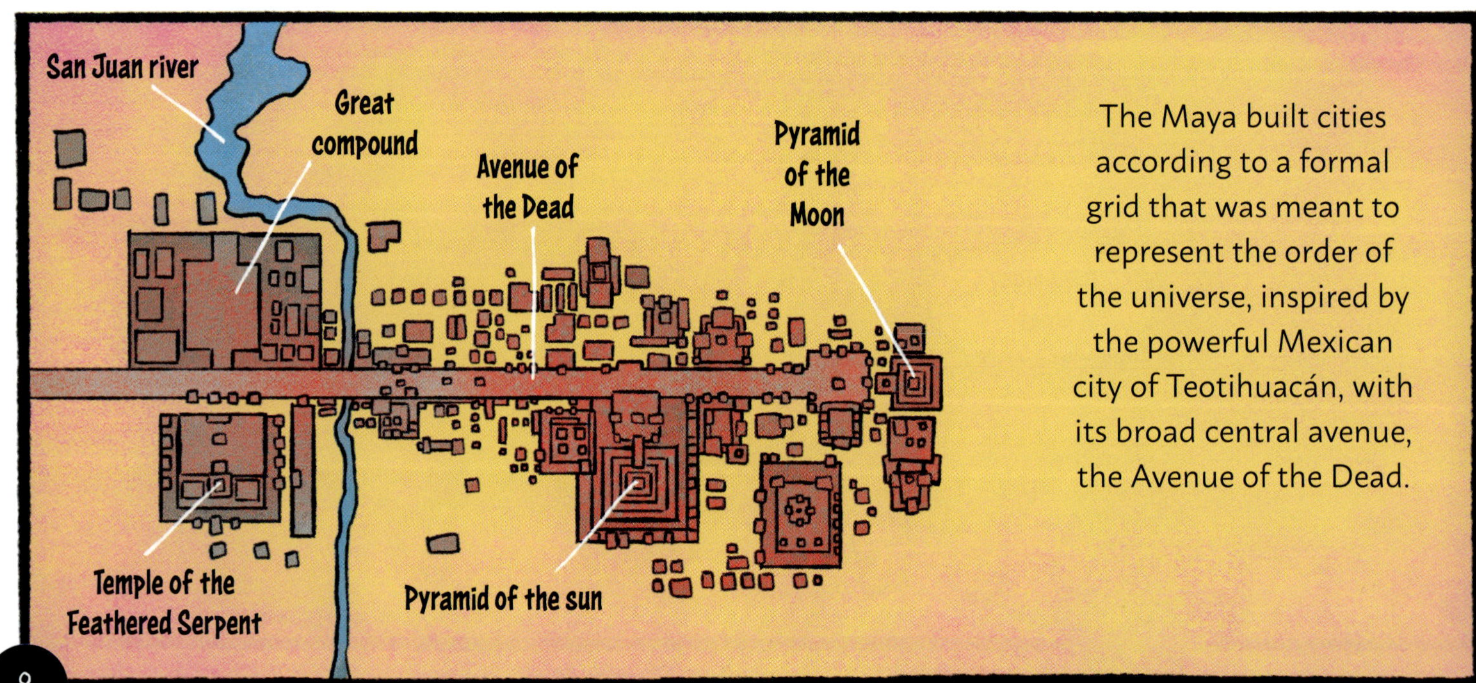

The Maya built cities according to a formal grid that was meant to represent the order of the universe, inspired by the powerful Mexican city of Teotihuacán, with its broad central avenue, the Avenue of the Dead.

A city center would be packed with impressive pyramids, temples, and palaces, which housed the royal family and religious leaders. Nearby were the administrative buildings and courts where ball games were played.

Homes belonging to the elite class were close to the center. Built from limestone, they were raised to avoid any risk of flooding. They were linked by stone walkways and often built as part of bigger complexes.

Further from the city center there were simpler homes built from lashed together wooden poles and adobe (mud and straw). The roof was thatched with palms to help the rain run off. On the edge of the city were the farmers' homes and fields.

WHO RULED THE MAYA?

Powerful kings (and queens) ruled over the city-states. They showed their importance by building awe-inspiring temples or pyramids. People worshipped their rulers like gods. In times of war, they commanded their fighting forces.

One of the most famous Maya rulers was Pakal I, also known as Pakal the Great, who ruled Palenque from 615 to 683 CE. He ordered the construction of some of the city's finest buildings and founded a great dynasty. He was only 12 when he became king.

At age 5 or 6, Maya princes had their first bloodletting (see page 15). Later, they went off to war to prove their bravery in battle.

When the existing ruler died or gave up the throne, the heir was made king at a special ceremony where he had to hold a scepter, wear a headdress of quetzal feathers and sit on a jaguar skin.

As ruler, the king had many religious duties to carry out. He had to be the link between his people and the gods. He also had to entertain visitors from other city-states.

The king was at the top of Maya society, along with his wives and children.

They were closely followed by the elite, who were royal relatives, administrators, generals, scribes, and priests.

Architects, craftspeople, merchants, and warriors came next . . .

. . . then the farmers and laborers.

Enslaved people came at the bottom of the heap. They did back-breaking building work or were given as sacrifices to the gods.

Who Were the Maya Gods?

The Maya had a rich mythology and worshipped many gods. Some took human form, others were animals, and some could shift between different forms and identities. The supreme god was Itzamna, the Maya creator god.

Lord of day and night and ruler of the heavens, Itzamna was said to have made humankind and devised its religious rituals, writing, and calendar. He was often depicted as a toothless old man with a crooked nose.

Itzamna's wife Ixchel was goddess of childbirth, healing, weaving, and the moon. Girls made offerings to her before they married. Ixchel was sometimes shown with jaguar ears or claws and wore a headdress with a snake curled around it.

Many gods looked after the weather and crops, which were vital to Maya survival.

Chac, the rain god, was a gentle warrior, who watered the crops with his tears.

The sun god, Kinich-Ahau, crossed the sky each day bringing warmth and light, but at night he took the form of a jaguar and turned into the fearsome god of darkness.

Skull-headed Ah Puch was associated with death.

The Maya believed he entered people's homes after dark and stole their souls.

At Chichén Itzá, people worshipped Kukulcan, the feathered serpent.

In a book called the *Popol Vuh*, the Maya described the universe as being made up of three layers: the underworld, the earth, and the upper realm, which was held up by Pauahtun, the god of thunder and wind.

Why Did the Maya Build Pyramids?

Tall, stepped pyramids were built to support Maya temples, holding them as close to the upper realm and the gods as possible. Some were also used as tombs, holding the remains of dead rulers deep within them.

Building pyramids was quite a feat. First, laborers piled up the central core of earth and rubble. Then they faced it with blocks of limestone, stuck together with a kind of plaster. The huge blocks of limestone were transported on log rollers.

Pyramid-top temples were the site of public ceremonies, carried out to keep the gods happy. Crowds of spectators gathered far below. Only rulers, priests, and sacrificial victims were allowed to climb the pyramid steps.

The Maya believed that their gods needed offerings of blood. One way to supply this was by sacrificing enslaved people, who were usually prisoners-of-war. Victims were beheaded with an axe or had their heart cut out while it was still beating.

Bloodletting was carried out upon kings and members of the elite. A spine from a stingray fish was used to pierce their tongue, lips, or ears, or they were cut with a stone knife. The Maya believed that the visions caused by the blood loss brought them closer to their ancestors and the gods.

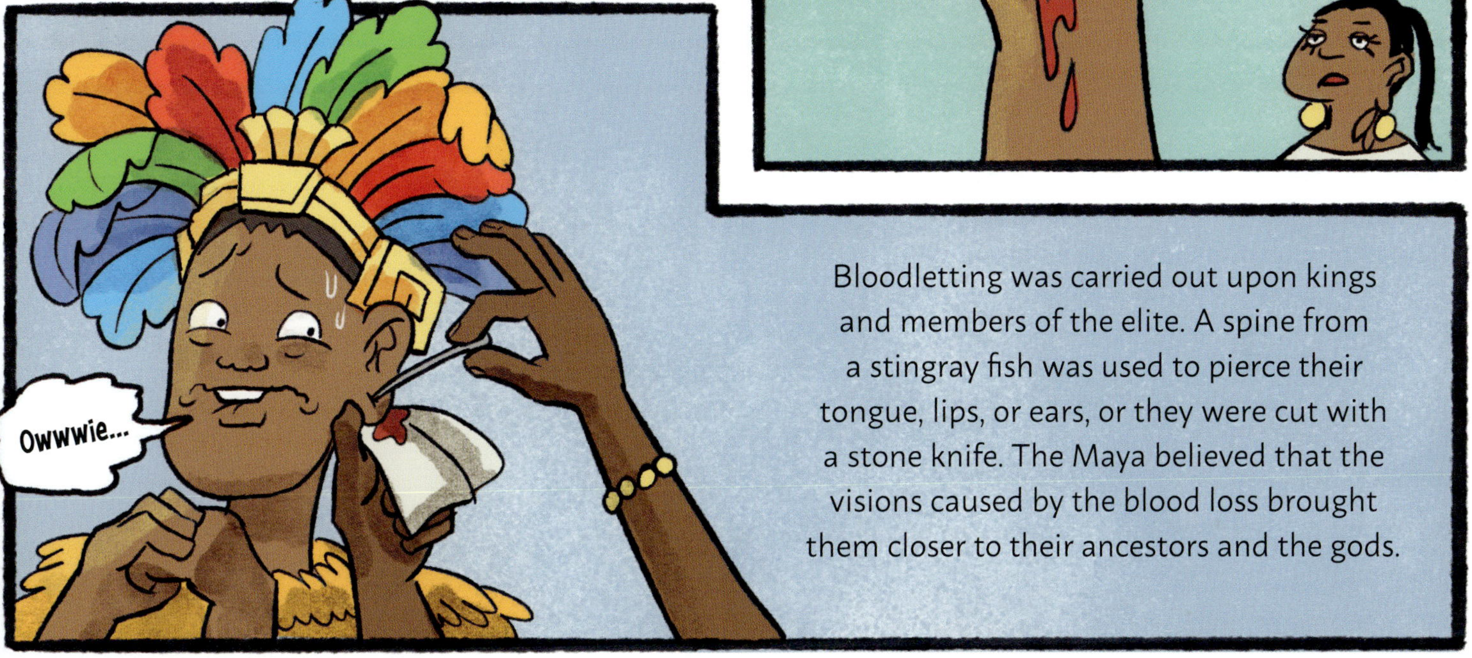

Ball courts were religious places, too, where players re-enacted ball games from the *Popol Vuh*. In real games, two teams passed a rubber ball around without using their hands and struck it through a stone hoop. Some experts believe that the winners (or losers) were rewarded with death.

WHAT WAS MAYA WRITING LIKE?

The Maya used symbols called hieroglyphs to write things down. These were painted on bark paper, wood, or pottery, or carved into stone. The earliest examples of Maya writing are stone inscriptions that date to the 200s BCE.

So far, we know of around 1,100 Maya hieroglyphs. These were usually read from left to right in a row and then top to bottom in a column. Some represented whole words or groups of words, and some represented sounds. Others were more like punctuation, indicating how the hieroglyphs should be read.

The Maya developed their own number system and a way of writing numbers down. They used just three symbols: a shell to mean zero, a dot for one, and a horizontal line to represent five. Three dots meant three, for example, while three lines meant 15.

Today, most cultures use a number system based on 10. From right to left, numbers represent units between zero and nine, then the quantity of tens, hundreds, thousands, and so on.

The Maya number system was based on 20, written from bottom to top. The bottom numeral was the number of units between zero and 19, the next indicated the quantities of 20s, then 400s, then 8,000s, and so on.

Scribes not only recorded events but also read sacred texts in order to advise the king. They probably passed on a basic knowledge of hieroglyphs and numbers to less important officials.

WHY DID THE MAYA STARGAZE?

Maya astronomers observed the movements of the sun, moon, Venus, and the stars. This knowledge helped the Maya to plan when to plant and harvest their crops, when to practice certain rituals and even when to fight wars.

They never discovered that the sun (not Earth) is at the center of the solar system, but Maya astronomers were able to predict astronomical events such as eclipses. They recorded their observations in two calendars: the 260-day sacred calendar called the *tzolk'in* and the 365-day solar *haab*.

The *tzolk'in* consisted of thirteen 20-day periods. Each day was represented by a particular animal, plant, or natural force and had its own hieroglyph. The *haab* was made up of eighteen 20-day periods plus a final period of five days, which were considered unlucky.

The Maya also recognized a period of time that they called a *baktun*, which amounted to just over 394 solar years.
The two Maya calendars interconnected so that every day had two name dates, one from the *haab* and one from the *tzolk'in*. Every 52 years, the first days of the *tzolk'in* and *haab* coincided.

The Maya used their knowledge of astronomy when planning their architecture. The circular building at Chichén Itzá known as El Caracol was positioned to line up with various important astronomical events, including the path of Venus. Venus was also important to the Maya because it was associated with war. Generals timed their battles to coincide with its "lucky" position in the sky.

How Did the Maya Dress?

Ordinary people and enslaved people wore plain loincloths, but the elite added feathers, animal skins, or gems as signs of status. Noblemen's headdresses were large and elaborate. Everyone wore sandals or went barefoot.

Noblemen wore a colorful garment that was a cross between a loincloth and a kilt, and wrapped a square cloak around their shoulders. Women dressed in a skirt and tunic.

Maya clothes were made from bark cloth, hemp, or cotton. Women colored the yarn first with plant or animal dyes, then wove it into cloth.

The Maya pierced their ears and put in heavy ear flares of jade or other precious stones. Elite men often had lip and nose plugs, too. They wore jewelry made of shells, jade beads, or jaguar fangs or claws.

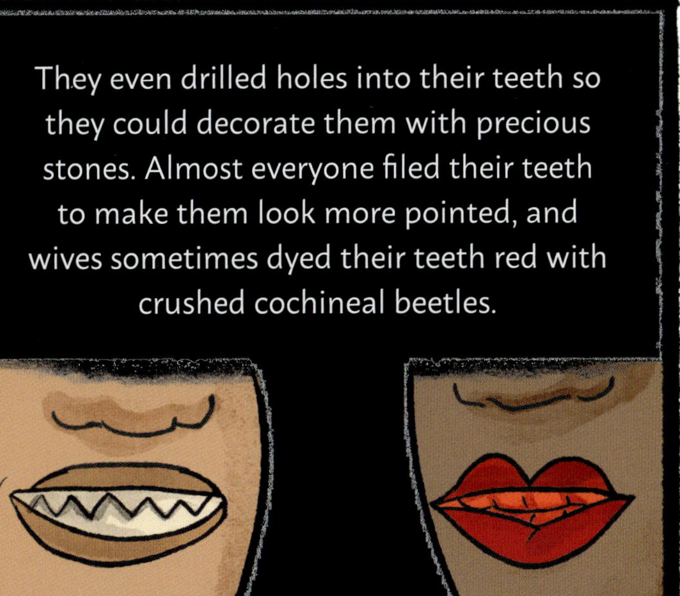

They even drilled holes into their teeth so they could decorate them with precious stones. Almost everyone filed their teeth to make them look more pointed, and wives sometimes dyed their teeth red with crushed cochineal beetles.

After marriage, some men and woman also had tattoos, although they were cut with a knife.

Body paint was common and less severe. Warriors favored patterns of black and red; priests painted themselves blue.

Talk about unrealistic beauty standards!
The Maya had surprising ideas of beauty: parents pressed their newborn babies' heads into a long shape between boards so that their child would look like the god of maize.

Parents also encouraged crossed eyes by dangling an object in front of their child's nose!

The Maya liked large noses. They stuffed objects into their nostrils to widen them.
Oh no! I think it's stuck!

What Art Did the Maya Make?

Maya art ranges from reliefs and sculptures to painted vases and murals. The Maya produced intricately detailed books and sculptors carved tall stone slabs, or stelae, that depicted Maya kings as divine beings.

The stonework of the most important Maya buildings was often beautifully carved, especially the lintels (stone doorways), wall panels, altars, or ball court hoops.

Artists also carved precious objects from jade, shell, and bone. Stucco (plasterwork) was molded to make bust portraits and raised friezes on walls.

The Maya made fine vessels for ritual use. They added ash, sand, or rock rubble to the raw clay to strengthen it, then shaped it by hand.

Once dry, the piece was inscribed, painted, or decorated using slip, a watery form of clay that has been colored with minerals, usually reds, creams, and blacks.

The Maya used illustrations and hieroglyphs on their vases to tell mythological stories. Once the vessel had been decorated, it was fired.

Maya artists used mineral paints to cover the walls of palaces, temples, tombs, and caves with striking frescoes. They produced scenes of divine and mythical creatures, battles, priests, nobles, and entertainers. The frescoes in the Temple of the Murals at Bonampak date from around 790 CE.

What Did Maya Merchants Trade?

The Maya were part of a large trading network. They drove their human caravans along roads, down rivers and around the coasts in order to trade, with fellow Maya and other peoples in their region.

Merchants had their own god, Ek Chuah, who was usually shown with a bundle of goods on his back.

Trade was essential for the Maya. No city-state was able to supply everything it needed for everyday life. Coastal Maya were rich in fish and salt but had no decent farmland so they needed to import maize and other crops.

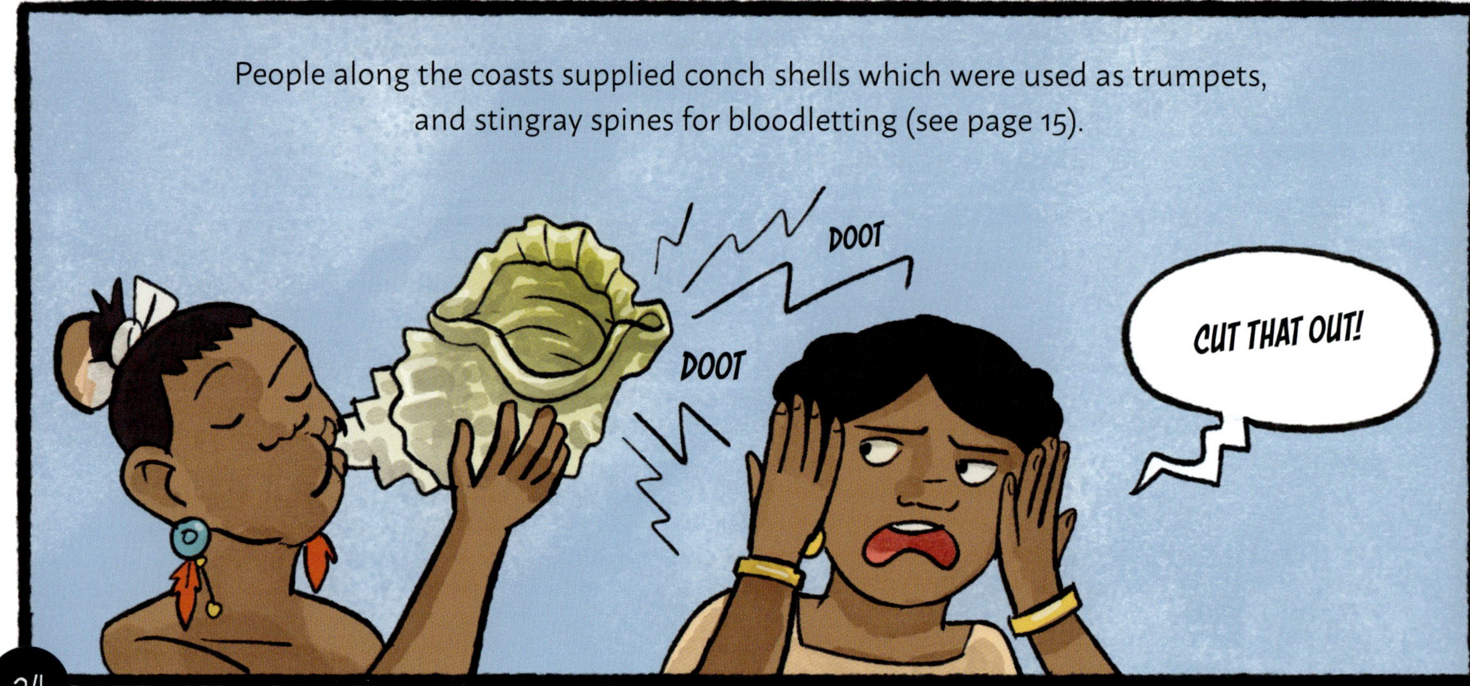

People along the coasts supplied conch shells which were used as trumpets, and stingray spines for bloodletting (see page 15).

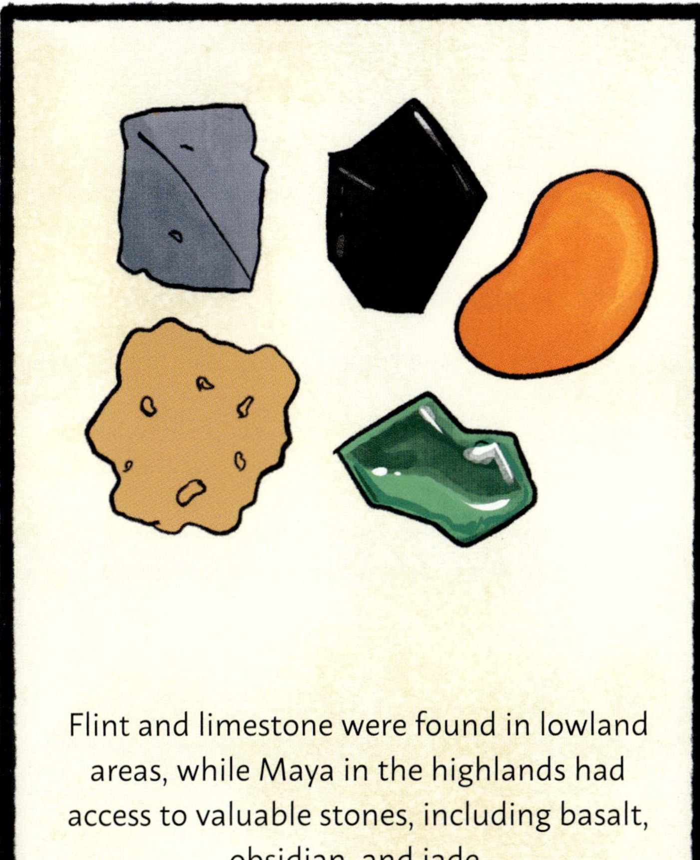

Flint and limestone were found in lowland areas, while Maya in the highlands had access to valuable stones, including basalt, obsidian, and jade.

The tropical lowlands were the place to find jaguar pelts, cacao beans, and pom (resin that was burned as incense). The highland forests were a source of quetzal feathers.

The Maya traded with paper (produced from fig-tree bark), books, furniture, jewelry, and textiles. The Maya simply bartered (swapped) what they had for basic items like food.

Luxurious items were sometimes paid for with valuable cacao beans, gold, or jade. When the Aztecs rose to power in central Mexico, the Maya exported dazzling green quetzal feathers, jaguar skins, and cacao to them in return for items made of copper.

What Happened to the Maya?

Around 900 CE, many city-states in the southern lowlands were abandoned, but this was not the end of Maya civilization. States in the uplands of the Yucatán peninsula continued to flourish until the arrival of the Spanish.

The Aztecs traded with the Maya and probably would have absorbed the last Maya cities into their own empire. However, before that could happen, Spanish explorers reached Central America.

The first contact between the Maya and Europeans happened in 1502. By the 1540s the Spanish controlled almost all Maya territory.

The Spanish forced the Maya to give up their own gods and become Christians. Father Diego de Landa arrived in the Yucatán in 1549 to help convert the Maya. He was responsible for burning many Maya books and figurines.

The Spanish also–without meaning to–brought diseases that the Maya had no immunity against.

The last city-states crumbled, but the people survived. Many headed into the forests to live again as slash-and-burn farmers, but some traded with the Europeans.

Today, millions of the descendants of the Maya live across Central America. The legacy of their ancestors lives on in all the wonderful architecture and artifacts they left behind.

Now you've learned all these facts about the Maya, why not try and discover even more?

Make your own model Maya pyramid. Have a look at examples from different sites and find a favorite to copy. Include a temple at the top, to reach the gods of the upper realm!

Find as many images of Maya rulers as you can, and then order them by date on a timeline. See if you can write their names in glyphs.

Look online for recipes using Maya ingredients and see if you can recreate any of their dishes. You could try making a Maya-style hot chocolate drink sprinkled with chili powder. Be very careful, though, a very small amount is hot and spicy!

Paint your own Maya fresco featuring Itzamna the creator god and his wife, Chac the rain god, Kinich-Ahau the sun god, Ah Puch the god of death, and Tohil the god of fire and sacrifice.

Make a Maya noblemen's headdress and decorate it with anything sparkling you can find to represent fine jewels and colorful feathers.

Set up a Maya ball game where both teams have to pass the ball around using only their knees, elbows, or hips, but never hands or feet. A team scores when a player manages to hit the ball through a hoop at each end, just like basketball.

Remember to do plenty of research. Use your local or school library, and look on the internet. Also check out the local museums to see what exhibitions they have.

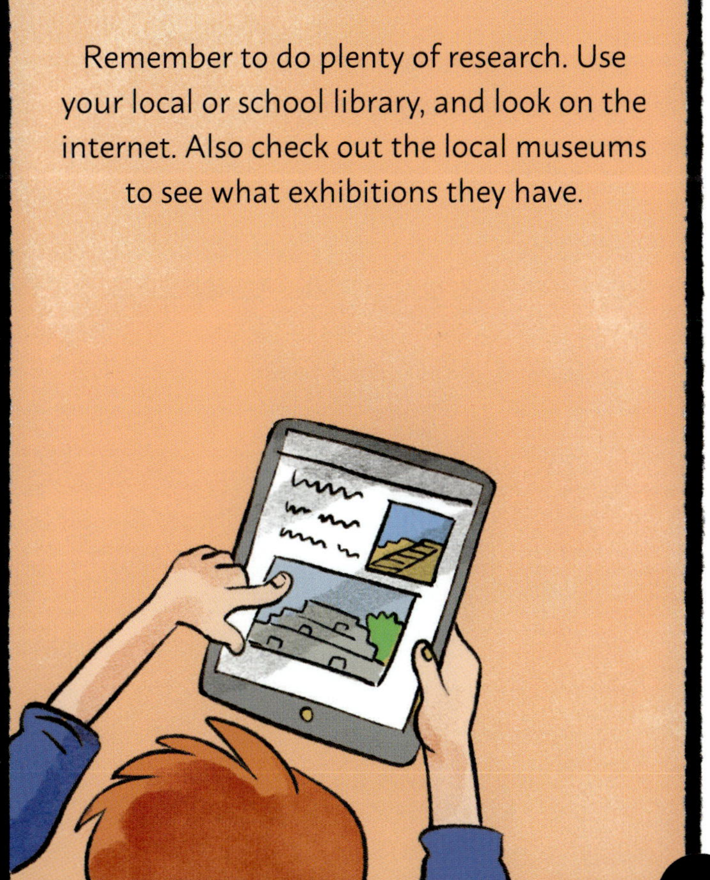

GLOSSARY

administrator Someone who helps to run something, for example a city-state.

archaeologist Someone who studies the remains of past societies.

astronomer Someone who studies the planets, stars, and universe.

bartered Traded by swapping goods, rather than using money.

BCE Stands for "Before Common Era." It's used to signify years before the birth of Jesus, around 2,000 years ago.

bloodletting A ritual that involves shedding a person's blood.

caravan A long line of people or animals traveling in single file.

cassava A plant with a starchy root.

CE Stands for "Common Era." It's used to signify years since the believed birth of Jesus.

city-state A self-governing, independent state consisting of a city and the surrounding area.

dynasty A ruling family.

ear flare A large, circular ear ornament, inserted into the pierced lobe of the ear and often made of jade.

elite In Maya society, the superior class of people that were second in importance only to the king.

fresco A painting on a freshly plastered wall.

hieroglyph A symbol used to represent a word or sound.

hunter-gatherer Someone who lives by hunting, fishing, and collecting wild foods.

immunity The ability to resist a particular disease.

lintel A stone block that forms the top of a doorway.

obsidian A glassy rock formed when volcanic lava cools.

pyramid A monument with a square base and sloping sides that meet at a point at the top.

quetzal Resplendent quetzal, a bird native to Central America, prized for its green tail feathers.

relief A carving that stands out or is raised from the surface.

resin A sticky, sometimes fragrant substance produced by trees.

slash-and-burn A way of clearing farmland, by slashing away most vegetation, then burning the rest.

stela (plural stelae) A tall, carved monumental stone.

Books to read

A Question of History: Why were Maya games so deadly? And Other Questions About the Maya by Tim Cooke (Franklin Watts, 2021)

Discovering the Technology of the Ancient Americas by Lindsey Lowe (Cavendish Square Publishing, 2024)

The Rise and Fall of the Maya Civilization by D. R. Faust (Bearport Publishing, 2025)

Websites

https://online.kidsdiscover.com/unit/the-maya

https://bedtimehistorystories.com/history-of-maya-civilization-for-kids/

Places to visit:

British Museum, London, UK

National Museum of Anthropology, Mexico City, Mexico

Peabody Museum, Cambridge, Massachusetts

Note to parents and teachers:

Every effort has been made by the publishers to ensure that these websites are suitable for children. However, because of the nature of the internet, it is impossible to guarantee that the contents of these sites will not be altered. We strongly advise that internet access is supervised by a responsible adult.

INDEX